Types of Business Entities

Steven M. Bragg

AccountingTools®

ISBN 978-1-64221-299-0

For more information about AccountingTools® products, visit our Web site at www.accountingtools.com.

Table of Contents

About the Author

Steven Bragg, CPA, has been the chief financial officer or controller of four companies, as well as a consulting manager at Ernst & Young. He received a master's degree in finance from Bentley College, an MBA from Babson College, and a Bachelor's degree in Economics from the University of Maine. He has been a two-time president of the Colorado Mountain Club, and is an avid alpine skier, mountain biker, and certified master diver. Mr. Bragg resides in Centennial, Colorado. He has written more than 300 books and courses, including *New Controller Guidebook*, *GAAP Guidebook*, and *Payroll Management*.

Steven maintains the accountingtools.com web site, which contains continuing professional education courses, the Accounting Best Practices podcast, and thousands of articles on accounting subjects.

Buy Additional AccountingTools Courses

AccountingTools offers more than 1,500 hours of CPE courses, with concentrations in accounting, auditing, finance, taxation, and ethics. Related courses that you might like include:

- C Corporation Tax Guide
- Essentials of Limited Liability Companies
- Partnership Taxation
- S Corporation Tax Guide

Go to accountingtools.com/cpe to view these additional courses.

AccountingTools®

Types of Business Entities

Introduction

When deciding which business type to use, it can be useful to compare the advantages and disadvantages of all main forms of organization, which include the following:

- Sole proprietorship
- General partnership
- Limited partnership
- Limited liability company
- C corporation
- S corporation

We do so in the following sections by describing the attributes of each of these forms of organization. At the end of the manual, we note the circumstances under which these business entities would be most useful.

Sole Proprietorship

A sole proprietorship is a business that is not incorporated; instead, it is merely an extension of the person who owns it. This means that the owner is entitled to the entire net worth of the business, and is personally liable for its debts. The business has no legal existence in the absence of the owner.

If the owner wants to operate the business under any name other than the person's legal name, then he or she should file a statement of trade name of an individual with the secretary of state of the applicable state government.

The individual and the business are considered to be the same entity for tax purposes, so the individual reports all business transactions on his or her individual income tax return. This means that a sole proprietorship is a pass-through entity, where earnings are subject to taxation at the level of the individual owner. The owner reports the income and expenses of the business on the Schedule C, which is filed along with the Form 1040. A separate Schedule C must be filed for each business owned by the taxpayer, and attached to the Form 1040.

Through 2025, a sole proprietor is entitled to a 20% business income deduction. The deduction is limited to 20% of the taxpayer's qualified business income, subject to several limitations. The deduction is not available for certain personal services businesses, such as accountants, attorneys, consultants, and doctors, above a certain taxable income cap that is adjusted each year.

It is generally allowable for a sole proprietor to use any losses from the business to offset other income. However, this will not be the case if the IRS determines that the sole proprietor is not engaging in the business for profit; if so, the individual can only deduct hobby expenses up to the amount of hobby income. A hobby loss cannot be deducted from other income.

A *hobby activity* is done mainly for recreation or pleasure. No one factor alone is decisive. One should consider the following factors in determining whether an activity is a business engaged in making a profit:

- Whether you carry on the activity in a businesslike manner and maintain complete and accurate books and records.
- Whether the time and effort you put into the activity indicates that you intend to make it profitable.
- Whether you depend on income from the activity for your livelihood.
- Whether your losses are due to circumstances beyond your control (or are normal in the startup phase of your type of business).
- Whether you change your methods of operation in an attempt to improve profitability.
- Whether you or your advisors have the knowledge needed to carry on the activity as a successful business.
- Whether you were successful in making a profit in similar activities in the past.
- Whether the activity makes a profit in some years and how much profit it makes.
- Whether you can expect to make a future profit from the appreciation of the assets used in the activity.

An activity is presumed to be carried on for profit if it produced a profit in at least three of the last five tax years, including the current year. The activity must be substantially the same for each year within this period. There is a profit when the gross income from an activity exceeds the deductions.

Deductions for hobby activities are claimed as itemized deductions on Schedule A (Form 1040). These deductions must be taken in the following order and only to the extent stated in each of three categories:

1. Deductions that a taxpayer may take for personal as well as business activities, such as home mortgage interest and taxes, may be taken in full.
2. Deductions that don't result in an adjustment to basis, such as advertising, insurance premiums and wages, may be taken next, to the extent gross income for the activity is more than the deductions from the first category.
3. Business deductions that reduce the basis of property, such as depreciation and amortization, are taken last, but only to the extent gross income for the activity is more than the deductions taken in the first two categories.

A sole proprietor needs to remit estimated tax payments to the government on a quarterly basis, which are based on both estimated federal income taxes and self-employment taxes. These payments are required if there is an expectation of owing at least $1,000 in taxes during the tax year.

If a sole proprietor elects to sell the business, the tax treatment is based on the sale of business assets, rather than the sale of an ownership interest in the business. This means that one must calculate a gain or loss on every asset sold as part of the sale transaction. To do so, each asset must be slotted into one of the following classifications and taxed at the rate noted for that classification:

1. Capital asset – taxed as a capital gain or loss. An example is goodwill.
2. Real property and depreciable property held for more than one year – taxed as a capital gain or loss. Examples are buildings and machinery.
3. Other property – taxed as an ordinary gain or loss. Examples are inventory and property held for one year or less.

Advantages and Disadvantages

The advantages of a sole proprietorship are:

- *Simple to organize.* The initial organization of the business is quite simple. At most, the owner might reserve a business name with the secretary of state. It is also quite easy to upgrade to other forms of organization.
- *Lower costs.* The accounting costs associated with a sole proprietorship tend to be quite low, since it is not necessary to maintain a separate set of books.
- *Simple tax filings.* The owner does not have to file a separate income tax return for the business. Instead, the results of the business are listed on a separate schedule of the individual income tax return (Form 1040).
- *No double taxation.* There is no double taxation, as can be the case in a corporation, where earnings are taxed at the corporate level and then distributed to owners via dividends, where they are taxed again. Instead, earnings flow straight to the owner.
- *Complete control.* There is only one owner, who has absolute control over the direction of the business and how its resources are allocated.
- *Withdrawals.* There is no tax effect when the owner transfers money to the business or removes money from it.

The disadvantages of a sole proprietorship are:

- *Unlimited liability.* The chief disadvantage is that the owner is entirely liable for any losses incurred by the business, with no limitation. For example, the owner may invest $1,000 in a real estate venture, which then incurs net obligations of $100,000. The owner is personally liable for the entire $100,000. An adequate amount of liability insurance and risk management practices can mitigate this concern.
- *Self-employment taxes.* The owner is liable for a 15.3% self-employment tax (social security and Medicare) on all earnings generated by the business that are not exempt from these taxes. There is a cap on the social security portion of this tax. There is no cap on the Medicare rate – instead, the rate increases by 0.9% at certain threshold levels.

- *No outside equity*. The only provider of equity to the business is the sole owner. Funding usually comes from personal savings and debt for which the owner is liable. For a large increase in capital, the owner would likely need to use a different organizational structure that would admit multiple owners.

The unlimited liability aspect of the sole proprietorship and the inability to bring in additional investors tends to limit its use to smaller organizations that require reduced levels of funding.

General Partnership

A partnership is a form of business organization to which the owners have made some sort of contribution (such as money, labor, or property) and from which they share in the resulting profits and losses. The partners have unlimited personal liability for the actions of the business, though this problem can be mitigated through the use of a limited liability partnership (see the next section). The owners of a partnership have invested their own funds and time in the business, and share proportionally in any profits earned by it, which are passed through to them. Thus, the partnership itself does not pay any income taxes; instead, income and losses are passed through to the partners, who are responsible for these payments, based on their own personal income tax brackets. The 20% business income deduction referred to earlier for sole proprietorships is also available to partners through 2025.

There is no limit on the number or types of partners in a partnership. Thus, an S corporation, a nonresident alien, and another partnership can be a partner. Also, it is allowable to have substantially more than 100 partners in a partnership.

A partnership is typically terminated through a winding up process, where the partnership collects all funds due to it from customers, pays off creditors, terminates any other liabilities, and pays any remaining funds to the partners in the business.

Family Partnerships

A sole proprietor may elect to form a partnership with other members of his or her family. If these new partners are being taxed at lower marginal income tax rates, then the aggregate result is a substantial reduction in the income taxes paid by the family as a whole. In short, some of the partnership's income is being shifted to family members with lower incomes, and who therefore pay a lower income tax rate. Given the tax advantages of this approach, the IRS is particularly watchful to see if any shares of partnership income are being routed to low-income partners who provide minimal service to the partnership. In particular, the IRS may impose the parent's marginal income tax rate on any partnership income allocated to a child, unless it can be proven that the child provided services to the partnership in exchange for the allocated income. Similarly, a purported gift of a partnership interest may be ignored if, in substance, the donor continues to own the interest through his or her power to control or influence the recipient's business decisions.

The IRS will recognize a family member as a partner in either of the following circumstances:

- When capital is a material income-producing factor in the partnership, and a family member acquires this capital interest in a legitimate transaction, such as by purchasing it or as a received gift; or
- When capital is not a material income-producing factor, but a family member is providing substantial services to the partnership.

The Partnership Agreement

There should be a partnership agreement which details the mechanics of how to make decisions, how to add new partners and pay off those who wish to leave, how to wind up the business, and so forth. However, it is not necessary to have a written partnership agreement. An oral one may be sufficient to prove the existence of a partnership. Common elements of a partnership agreement include the following:

- The ownership percentage assigned to each partner. If this is not clearly stated in the agreement, then the ownership percentage is considered to be based on the proportions of capital paid into the partnership. If there is a change in ownership during the tax year, then the average share must be calculated for each owner for tax purposes, though this can be overridden by other terms in the agreement.
- Each partner's share of income, gains, losses, deductions, and credits. However, these allocations will be disregarded if they do not have a substantial economic effect. An allocation has a substantial economic effect when both of the following are true:
  - There is a reasonable possibility that the allocation will substantially impact the dollar amount of the partners' shares of partnership income or loss independently of tax consequences; and
  - The partner receiving the allocation actually receives it or bears the economic burden associated with it.

  When there is no substantial economic effect, a partner's distribution is based on the individual's ownership interest in the partnership.

- The situations in which the partners can buy out another partner, and how the payment is to be calculated and made.
- The amounts of any preferential payments to certain partners.

This agreement may be modified for a stated tax year after the close of that tax year, but no later than the filing date for the partnership's tax return.

Partnership Elections

Partners can make several elections that impact the amount of taxable income recognized by a partnership, because they alter the timing of either revenue or expense recognition. These elections are:

- Record transactions under either the cash, accrual, or hybrid methods of accounting
- Select the type of depreciation method used
- Select the methods to be used to recognize revenue

Original Basis and Adjusted Basis

When a partner acquires an interest in a partnership, the original basis of that interest is the amount of any money contributed by the partner, as well as the adjusted basis of any contributed property. There are a number of ways to adjust this original basis. Increases to it can be accomplished by either of the following actions:

- Additional contributions to the partnership
- Distributive shares of the partnership's taxable and non-taxable income

Decreases of original basis down to a minimum threshold of zero can be triggered by any of the following items:

- Any distributive shares of the partnership's losses
- Any funds distributed by the partnership to the partner
- Any nondeductible partnership expenses not classified as capital expenditures
- The adjusted basis of any property distributed by the partnership to the partner

Inside Basis vs. Outside Basis

When dealing with partnerships, one should understand the difference between the two types of tax bases. The *inside basis* is the partnership's tax basis in individual assets. The *outside basis* is the tax basis of each individual partner's interest in the partnership. When a partner contributes property to the partnership, the partnership's basis in the contributed property is equal to its fair market value. However, the outside basis of the partner increases only by the amount of the basis that the partner had in the property.

EXAMPLE

Mr. Smith contributes land to a partnership with a tax basis of $10,000 and fair market value of $50,000. Mr. Jones contributes $50,000 cash. Since the fair market value of the land is also $50,000, the two men have equal equity in the partnership, and the total inside basis of the partnership is equal to $100,000. However, Mr. Smith's outside basis differs from that of Mr. Jones, since the outside basis of Mr. Smith is $10,000, while that of Mr. Jones is $50,000. If Mr. Smith were to sell his partnership interest for $50,000, he would recognize a gain of $40,000, while Mr. Jones, if he were to sell at the same price, would recognize no gain.

An increase in a partnership's liabilities increases the outside basis of its partners, as though they had contributed cash to the entity. Conversely, a decline in a partnership's liabilities decreases the outside basis of its partners, as though the partnership had distributed cash to them.

Partnership Taxation

The primary tax form filed by a partnership is the Form 1065, which is an information return. This form notes the amount of taxable income generated by the partnership, and the amount of this income attributable to each of the partners (which includes any guaranteed salary or interest payments). In addition, the partnership issues a Schedule K-1 to each of the partners, on which is stated the amount of partnership income attributed to them as of the last day of the partnership's tax year, and which they should include on their own Form 1040 personal income tax returns. The form must be filed by March 15 following a calendar-year close. If a partnership operates on a different fiscal year, then it must file the return by the 15th day of the third month after its year-end.

A partner is taxed on his or her share of partnership income, even if this income is not distributed to the partner. In effect, this income is taxed when *earned*, rather than when *distributed*. This typically means that partners require some distribution of cash from the partnership in order to pay their taxes. If a partner elects to instead leave some portion of his or her share of a distribution in the partnership, this is considered an incremental increase in the capital contribution of that person to the business.

Each partner should separately record his or her share of certain partnership items, which are broken out from all other partnership transactions. This separate recordation is needed in order to determine a partner's federal income tax. Items requiring separate recordation include gains and losses from the sale of capital assets, charitable contributions, recoveries of bad debts, and any items such as a special allocation under the terms of the partnership agreement. These items must be separately recorded, since their tax impact on partners will vary, depending on the circumstances of each partner.

In those instances where a partnership recognizes a loss during its fiscal year, the share of the loss recognized by each partner in his or her personal tax return is limited to the amount of the loss that offsets each partner's outside basis in the partnership. If the amount of the loss is greater than this basis, the excess amount must be carried forward into a future period, where it can hopefully be offset against the future profits of the partnership. In essence, tax law does not allow a partner to recognize more on his or her tax return than the amount contributed into a partnership.

Note: A partner's basis in a partnership is increased by his or her share of the partnership's income and tax-exempt income, while it is decreased by his or her share of the partnership's losses.

If a partner has not yet paid for his or her interest in a partnership, and no other events have occurred to increase his or her basis, then that partner cannot recognize any part of his or her share of the partnership's losses until a later year when the person's basis increases above zero.

A partner is required to make quarterly estimated income tax payments. This payment can be the lesser of 90% of the partner's share of the partnership's expected annual income, or 100% of the actual tax paid in the immediately preceding year. The partnership itself is not subject to federal income tax.

A final tax issue is that partners are not considered to be employees of a partnership, and so must remit the full amount of the self-employment tax.

> **Note:** A penalty is assessed against a partnership if it is required to file a partnership return and it (a) fails to file the return by the due date, including extensions, or (b) files a return that fails to show all the information required, unless the failure is due to reasonable cause. The penalty is $210 for each month or part of a month (for a maximum of 12 months) the failure continues, multiplied by the total number of persons who were partners in the partnership during any part of the partnership's tax year for which the return is due.
>
> For each failure to furnish Schedule K-1 to a partner when due and each failure to include on Schedule K-1 all the information required to be shown (or the inclusion of incorrect information), a $280 penalty may be imposed for each Schedule K-1 for which a failure occurs.

Partnership Tax Year

Partnerships are usually required to use the calendar year as their fiscal year, unless there is a business purpose for using a different fiscal year. A partnership using a different fiscal year must pay the IRS a deposit; this is intended to approximate the amount of tax that would be paid if the partnership changed to a calendar year; thus, the payments offset the income tax deferral provided by the fiscal year.

Guaranteed Payments

A partnership may agree to pay a salary to a partner. This guaranteed payment is considered to be income to the partner, and may be a valid business expense for the partnership. These payments are treated as the recipient's distribution of the partnership's ordinary income for tax purposes. As such, they are included in the partnership's Schedule K-1 and in the Form 1040 of the partner.

Contributed Services

A partner may acquire an interest in a partnership based on services performed on behalf of the partnership. For example, a person could agree to work 1,000 hours for a partnership for free, in exchange for a 10% interest in the entity. When this is the case, the partner is considered to have received taxable income on the value of the partnership interest granted to him or her in exchange for providing services to the partnership. The fair market value of this partnership interest is considered to be a guaranteed payment.

> **Tip:** A way to avoid the immediate taxability of a partnership interest issued in exchange for services rendered is to instead give the individual an interest in the *future* profits of the partnership. Doing so means that the partner will not be taxed until he or she receives profits from the partnership.

Property Contributions

A partner may contribute property to a partnership in order to acquire a partnership interest. When this happens, the partner cannot recognize a gain or loss on the contribution. However, if the partner were to sell the property to the partnership, then he or she could recognize a gain or loss on the transaction. If the partner were to recognize a loss on this sale, it would be disallowed if the partner owns more than 50% of the partnership.

Related-Party Transactions

In cases where a partner sells assets to the partnership, it is normally treated as an arm's-length transaction between unrelated parties. However, when the partner owns more than 50% of the partnership, he or she cannot take a deduction on a loss on the sale. Also, if this partner were to instead recognize a gain on the asset sale to the partnership, then the partner must treat the gain as ordinary income, instead of a capital gain.

Sale or Exchange of Partnership Interests

An interest in a partnership is classified as a capital asset. When a partner sells or exchanges his or her partnership interest, this results in the recognition of a gain or loss on the transaction. The amount of the gain or loss is calculated as the difference between the amount realized from the sale or exchange and the partner's adjusted basis in the partnership interest. In most instances, the outcome is treated as a capital gain or loss. However, the consideration allocable to *hot assets* is treated as ordinary income. Hot assets are accounts receivable not already recognized as income, LIFO reserves, appreciated inventory, and depreciation recapture. Thus, a selling partner's tax treatment depends on the underlying partnership assets.

When the person purchasing a partnership interest assumes partnership liabilities, this counts as a portion of the consideration paid to acquire the partnership interest.

Partnership Distributions

The distribution of cash property from a partnership to its partners is not normally considered to be a taxable event, either on the part of the partnership or the partner. However, taxable events will arise in the following situations:

- When the cash distributed exceeds the adjusted basis of a partner's interest, triggering recognition of a gain.
- When a distribution liquidates a partner's interest, and the distribution is less than the adjusted basis of the partner's interest.

Partnership Liquidations

When a partnership liquidates, only those partners who receive a liquidating distribution of cash may have an immediate taxable gain or loss. The value of marketable securities and decreases to a partner's share of the partnership's debt are both treated as cash distributions.

When the total amount of cash distributed is more than a partner's basis in his or her partnership interest, the difference is a gain. Conversely, when the total amount of cash distributed is less than the partner's basis, the difference is classified as a loss. However, a partner can only recognize a taxable loss when it is solely the result of a liquidating distribution of cash, outstanding partnership receivables, or inventory items.

If a partnership distributes property to its partners as part of a liquidation, there is no immediate tax effect. Instead, the related gain or loss is deferred until the property is eventually sold. A partner's tax basis in distributed property is equal to his or her adjusted basis in the partnership interest, minus any distributed cash. If this basis is zero, then the amount for which the property is eventually sold is all taxable gain.

Once a partnership liquidates, the IRS views distributions to partners as the sale of a partnership interest. As a result, gains are usually taxed as long-term capital gains to partners. Consequently, partners who have held an interest in the partnership for more than a year will pay lower tax rates on any gains recognized than is the case with their share of a partnership's operating profit.

Partnership Termination

When a partnership is terminated, all income or loss incurred through the termination date must be included in the tax returns of the partners within that same year. In addition, all assets of the partnership are deemed to have been distributed to the partners as soon as it is terminated.

A variation on the concept arises when one partner of a two-partner firm leaves it or dies; in this case, the partnership is considered to still be in existence until the partnership has made all payments to the partner who left or died.

Advantages and Disadvantages

The advantages of a partnership are:

- *Source of capital*. With many partners, a business has a much richer source of capital than would be the case for a sole proprietorship.
- *Classes of ownership*. There can be more than one class of partnership interests.
- *Specialization*. If there is more than one general partner, it is possible for multiple people with diverse skill sets to run a business, which can enhance its overall performance. In general, this may mean that there is more expertise within the business.
- *Minimal tax filings*. The Form 1065 that a partnership must file is not a complicated tax filing.
- *No double taxation*. There is no double taxation, as can be the case in a corporation.
- *Special allocations*. The partnership agreement can state special partner allocations that differ from the respective ownership interests of the partners.
- *Pass-through*. Income, losses and credits are passed through to the partners for taxation purposes.
- *Family benefits*. Family partnerships can be used to reduce the aggregate tax liability across a family.

The disadvantages of a partnership are:

- *Unlimited liability*. The partners have unlimited personal liability for the obligations of the partnership, as was the case with a sole proprietorship. This is a *joint and several liability*, which means that creditors can pursue a single general partner for the obligations of the entire business.
- *Taxed on undistributed earnings*. The partners are taxed on the current earnings of the partnership, even if those earnings are not distributed to them. This can cause problems when the partnership needs to retain the cash to support operations, while the partners need it to pay taxes.
- *Multiple tax filings*. When the partnership spans multiple states, partners may have to file individual state income tax returns in all of those states.
- *Self-employment taxes*. A partner's share of the ordinary income reported on a Schedule K-1 is subject to the self-employment tax. This is a 15.3% tax (social security and Medicare) on all profits generated by the business that are not exempt from these taxes.

Limited Partnership

A limited partnership is an organizational structure in which certain partners can only lose the amount of their investments. These investors, known as limited partners, are not liable for any additional losses suffered by the partnership beyond the amount of their investments. In exchange for this limited liability, limited partners have no control over the management direction of the entity. The general partner who runs the partnership is liable for the full extent of the entity's losses.

This organizational structure mixes some aspects of a corporation (with its limited liability for limited partners) and partnerships (with its unlimited liability for the general partner). A limited liability partnership must have a formal agreement between the partners, so that the limited and general partners can be clearly identified. For tax purposes, this arrangement is a pass-through entity, where the partners are responsible for paying income taxes, rather than the entity.

There can be an unlimited number of limited partners in a limited partnership, and any type of entity can be a limited partner. Also, the general partner can be in a form other than an individual, such as an S corporation.

From the perspective of the limited partner, the main concern with this structure is that they have no voting control over management decisions, which are entirely up to the general partner.

Advantages and Disadvantages

The main advantage of a limited partnership is that the liability of limited partners is restricted to their investment in the partnership. The disadvantages of a limited partnership are:

- The general partner has unlimited liability.
- The limited partners have no voting control over management decisions.

C Corporation

A C corporation uses a corporate structure that is taxed directly, rather than passing income through to its owners for taxation purposes. This tax structure is useful, in that the flat 21% corporate tax rate is substantially less than the tax rate charged to high-income individuals. Since less cash is paid to the government, a C corporation has more cash available for other purposes, such as reinvesting profits in the business. Also, since it has a corporate structure, its owners do not incur any liabilities taken on by the corporation, and so are not liable to its creditors. Another benefit is that a C corporation can survive its owners, persisting as new owners take the place of the old ones. Yet another advantage is that the entity can issue a variety of types of stock, such as several classes of preferred stock, which allows it to raise money more easily than other legal forms of business. Furthermore, anyone can be a shareholder, including nonresident aliens, trusts, estates, another C corporation, and so forth. An essential advantage of a C corporation is the free transferability of interests, where a shareholder's interest in the corporation (a stock certificate) can be sold to another party.

The single largest complaint about the C corporation is the concept of double taxation. In essence, the corporation is taxed on its earnings, while its shareholders are taxed again when they receive dividends from the corporation. This issue can be reduced when shareholders are also employees, by paying them a salary instead of dividends (though doing so will incur payroll taxes).

A C corporation is formed by registering with the secretary of state's office for the applicable state, and issuing stock certificates to its owners. The shareholders then elect a board of directors, which governs the entity in their stead. The board hires a management team, which runs the business for them. The corporate secretary is also responsible for filing an annual report with the secretary of state's office for as long as the entity remains in business.

Personal Service Corporations

A personal service corporation is one that performs services in any of the following fields: accounting, architecture, actuarial science, consulting, health care, law, or the performing arts. At least 20% of these services must be performed by the employee-owners, who own more than 10% of the entity's stock. Also, more than half of its total compensation costs should be for personal service activities. The employee-owner designation implies that these entities are relatively small.

This entity is useful to high-earning professionals, since the C corporation structure allows employee/owners to leave some of their earnings in the corporation, which means that it will be taxed at the lower 21% corporate rate, rather than their higher marginal tax rates. They can also take advantage of the limited liability afforded by a C corporation, as well as the tax-deductibility of fringe benefits paid on their behalf by the corporation.

A personal service corporation is generally required to use a calendar tax year, unless it can justify a different period with a valid business purpose.

Note: The owners of a personal service corporation do not want to have it characterized as a personal holding company, which would trigger the imposition of a 20% penalty tax on undistributed income. The best way to avoid this penalty is to limit the amount of undistributed income in the business.

Start-Up Expenses

A C corporation can deduct up to $5,000 of its start-up costs in the taxable year in which the entity begins. This deduction is reduced dollar-for-dollar (but not below zero) by the cumulative amount of start-up costs exceeding $50,000. The remaining start-up costs can be deducted ratably over a 15-year period, beginning with the month in which the active trade[1] or business begins.

Start-up costs are those costs paid or incurred in connection with investigating the creation or acquisition of an active trade or business, or creating an active trade or business. These costs include amounts paid or incurred in connection with an existing activity engaged in for profit, and for the production of income in anticipation of the activity becoming an active trade or business. Expenditures that would otherwise have been capitalized, such as the costs associated with the construction of a capital asset, are not startup costs.

---

[1] Active trade occurs when a corporation has begun the conduct of operations for which it was organized. That is, it is in a position to begin generating revenue.

Expenses related to investigating the creation or acquisition of a trade or business are known as *investigatory expenses*. They are the costs incurred in searching for and analyzing prospective businesses prior to making a final decision about whether to acquire an existing business, create a new business, or forego a business transaction. These costs may be treated as deductible or amortizable startup costs only if they would be currently deductible by an existing trade or business in the same field. Deductible investigatory expenses include costs incurred for the analysis or survey of potential markets, products, labor supply, and transportation facilities.

Expenses of creating an active business are costs incurred after the investigatory process has determined that a particular business should be acquired or established, but not before the business actually begins operations. Examples of these costs are advertising expenses, wages paid to trainee employees and their instructors, travel expenses incurred to line up prospective business partners, and fees paid for consultants and professional services.

Other start-up expenses may include the following:

- Business investigation expenses, such as surveys, market studies, and consulting fees
- Pre-opening advertising and promotional efforts
- Travel expenses for efforts to find a location or secure suppliers or customers
- Salaries, employee benefits, insurance, and overhead
- Pre-opening repair and maintenance of capital assets to be used in the business
- Mortgage standby commitment fees to ensure financing for the new venture
- Accounting and legal fees that are not organizational costs
- Employee training
- Rent and utilities for space maintained during the pre-opening phase
- Costs of expanding an existing business or beginning a new business if a new entity is used

Organizational Expenses

When a C corporation has been newly organized, it may choose to defer its organizational expenses and amortize them over a period of time. The entity can deduct up to $5,000 of organizational expenditures in the tax year in which the trade or business is initiated. As was the case with start-up expenses, the $5,000 is reduced (but not below zero) by the cumulative amount of organizational costs exceeding $50,000. The remaining start-up costs can be deducted ratably over a 15-year period, beginning with the month in which the active trade or business begins.

Examples of organizational expenses are incorporation fees, and fees paid to draft the charter and bylaws of a business, as well as the terms of its original stock certificates.

Inventory Treatment

If a C corporation has inventory, then it must use the *accrual basis* of accounting, where accounting transactions for revenue are recorded when earned and expenses when they are incurred. In addition, the accountant must determine the value of the inventory at the beginning and end of the tax year, since this is a key component of the taxable income calculation. Also, the business must consistently employ an inventory identification method, of which the following are commonly used:

- *First in, first out method (FIFO)*. This approach incorporates the assumption that the first items to enter inventory are the first ones used or sold. This means that inventory items still on hand at year-end are valued at the cost of the most recently purchased items.
- *Last in, first out method (LIFO)*. This approach incorporates the assumption that the last items to enter inventory are the first ones used or sold. This means that inventory items still on hand at year-end are assumed to have been in inventory at the beginning of the tax year, adjusted for any changes since then.
- *Specific identification method*. This approach involves assigning a cost to each specific unit of inventory, and is typically only used for unique inventory items, such as watches, paintings, and vehicles.

Corporations tend to prefer the LIFO method during periods of rising prices, since it tends to result in an increased ending inventory valuation, which leads to a reduced amount of taxable income. Conversely, the FIFO method is the better choice during a period of declining prices, since this results in the higher ending inventory valuation, and therefore the lowest amount of taxable income.

Costs assigned to inventory items are the cost of the raw materials, components, and merchandise purchased, in addition to costs that are reasonably allocable to them. This typically means that the cost of inventory is comprised of the invoice price, minus any discounts, plus transportation costs, tariffs, and other fees. The costs assigned to manufactured goods include the cost of raw materials and production supplies used in the production process, as well as the costs of direct labor and any reasonably allocable factory overhead charges.

> **Note:** The capitalization of certain costs into inventory is governed by the Uniform Capitalization rules of the IRS, which require a business to capitalize the direct and indirect costs of inventory, including both those inventory items that were produced and those that were acquired for resale. In particular, the rules mandate that all costs that can be attributed to creating or acquiring items of inventory be included in the cost of inventory, rather than being claimed as a current deduction. These costs will eventually be deducted when the inventory is sold or otherwise disposed of.

Capital Gains and Losses

A C corporation can only deduct its capital losses up to the amount of any capital gains it has realized in the tax year. Any excess capital loss must be carried back or carried forward to other tax years and offset against any capital gains occurring in those years. These excess capital losses may be carried back three years and carried forward five years.

Dividends Received Deduction

A C corporation can deduct 50% of the dividends it receives from a domestic corporation, as long as the firm owns less than 20% of the business issuing the dividends. Thus, a business that receives $10,000 in dividends can deduct half of this amount from its gross income. Theoretically, if a C corporation's entire income were derived from such dividends, this deduction would reduce its effective federal income tax from 21% to 10.5%.

The deduction is 65% when the dividends received are from a company that is at least 20% owned by the receiving entity.

The dividends received deduction is intended to alleviate the potential consequences of triple taxation; this occurs when the same income is taxed in the hands of the company paying the dividend, then in the hands of the company receiving the dividend, and again when the ultimate shareholder is, in turn, paid a dividend.

Charitable Contributions

A C corporation can claim a deduction for any charitable contributions made to a 501(c)(3) nonprofit entity. These deductions are limited to 10% of the firm's taxable income.

Accumulated Earnings Tax

If a C corporation builds up its earnings beyond the reasonable needs of the business, it could be subject to an accumulated earnings tax, which is 20% of accumulated taxable income. If the IRS deems this tax to be applicable, then it will also impose interest on tax underpayments from the date when the entity's corporate return was originally due.

> **Note:** It is acceptable for most corporations to accumulate earnings of at least $250,000 without having to justify it with a specific business purpose. This amount is reduced to $150,000 for personal service corporations.

Corporation Termination

When a corporation is dissolved, it sells off its assets, settles all remaining obligations, and issues a liquidating distribution to its shareholders. This distribution is treated as being an exchange for their stock. The amount of cash received by a shareholder, plus the value of any property received, minus the shareholder's basis in the stock, is a capital gain or loss.

Tax Return

The federal tax return of a C corporation is the Form 1120, which must be filed by the 15th day of the fourth month after its tax year ends.

Advantages and Disadvantages

The advantages of a C corporation are:

- *Tax rate*. It is subject to a flat 21% income tax rate.
- *Liability shield*. Shareholders are not liable for the obligations of the corporation.
- *Fringe benefits*. It can deduct the cost of any fringe benefits it pays to any shareholders who are also employees. Examples of these benefits are medical insurance, life insurance, and disability insurance.
- *Dividends received deduction*. It pays a reduced tax on dividends received from other entities, subject to certain restrictions.
- *Multiple stock classes*. It can issue multiple classes of stock in order to attract investors with differing requirements.
- *Shareholders allowed*. Any entity can be a shareholder of a C corporation, including ones barred from owning an S corporation.
- *Transferable shares*. Depending on whether shares are restricted, it is relatively easy for parties to buy and sell shares in a C corporation.
- *Fiscal year*. It can set its own fiscal year, rather than being forced to use the calendar year.

The disadvantages of a C corporation are:

- *Double taxation*. Its earnings are taxed when earned, while any dividends issued are taxable to the receiving shareholders.
- *Accumulated earnings tax*. It may be liable for an accumulated earnings tax, if it builds its earnings beyond the reasonable needs of the business.

Limited Liability Company

A limited liability company (LLC) is a business entity that provides its owners (known as members[2]) with the limited liability protection of a corporation, while allowing earnings to pass through to the members for tax purposes. Thus, an LLC combines the best features of a corporation and a partnership while not being classified as either one. An LLC is created by state statute, and is usually taxable as a partnership under federal tax law. However, LLC law may differ by state, and may not exist at all in some states, which presents a concern that the liability protections afforded by this structure may not be valid in certain states.

---

[2] A member is an individual or entity holding a membership interest in an LLC. Members are the owners of an LLC, like shareholders are the owners of a corporation. Initial members are

> **Note:** An LLC is formed by filing articles of incorporation. Prior to the filing date, members are liable for any obligations incurred by the entity.

A member's basis in an LLC is increased by the entity's profits and decreased by its losses. This differs from the situation with a C corporation, where the basis of shareholders is not impacted by the profits or losses of the corporation.

When an LLC is taxed as a partnership, an increase in the LLC's liabilities is treated as a cash contribution by its members, which gives them a higher tax basis. Having a higher basis allows a member to deduct more losses passed through from the LLC, as well as to receive more tax-free distributions from the LLC.

An LLC is frequently used when there are few members, or just one member. However, there is no limitation on the number or type of members, so there could be more than 100, and a nonresident alien or a trust can be a member.

A possible concern is that an LLC must have the same tax year as its members, which generally restricts it to having a calendar year.

An LLC is allowed to have multiple classes of stock, which allows it to provide different rights to different groups of shareholders.

There are several estate and income tax planning advantages to using an LLC, which are as follows:

- *Flexible allocation of income.* The members can enter into an LLC operating agreement that specifies how taxable income and losses are to be allocated among the members. This approach differs from an S corporation, where allocations are strictly on a per-share basis.
- *Use of debt basis.* The liabilities of the LLC are considered to be contributions of the members, which means that LLC debt increases member basis. This does not happen in an S corporation, unless a shareholder directly lends assets to the corporation.

An LLC has a clear advantage over a C corporation in the matter of compensation. The IRS can disallow a salary paid to a shareholder as being unreasonable compensation, so that it is instead taxed as a dividend. This is not the case with an LLC, where the IRS does not care if a member is paid via a distributive share of income or via a salary.

An LLC is not allowed in some states for certain purposes, such as the provision of professional services. Or, a state may impose certain requirements on the members when professional services are being offered, such as not being able to exempt themselves from liability for their own malpractice.

---

admitted at the time of formation. Additional members may be admitted based on the conditions set forth in the operating agreement.

Advantages and Disadvantages

The advantages of a limited liability company are:

- *Active participation*. Members can actively participate in the management of the business, which is not the case with a limited partnership. This means that there is no need to designate a general partner to run the business.
- *Limited liability*. Members are not personally liable for the debts of the business, which is not the case with a partnership.
- *Earnings pass-through*. If the entity is taxed as a partnership, then its earnings are passed through to its members. This differs from the double-taxation situation that applies to C corporations.
- *No member restrictions*. There are no restrictions on the number or type of members in the business, which is not the case with an S corporation. This means that a nonresident alien can be a member of an LLC, which is not possible in an S corporation.
- *Unique rights*. Special rights can be set up to favor some members over others in the allocation of taxable income and losses. In addition, these rights can be adjusted by altering the LLC's operating agreement.
- *Multiple classes of stock*. An LLC can issue multiple classes of stock, which gives it the opportunity to provide different rights to different groups of shareholders.

The disadvantages of a limited liability company are:

- *State specific*. The laws concerning LLCs are at the state level, and there are differences between state laws (or there are no laws at all). A possible outcome is that an LLC established in one state may lose its liability protection if it operates in another state that has no LLC statute, or one with different laws.
- *Restrictions on use*. Some states specifically restrict the types of businesses that can use the LLC structure.
- *Self-employment tax*. When a member is actively engaged in managing an LLC, that person is subject to the self-employment tax, which is a 15.3% tax (including social security and Medicare).

S Corporation

A central problem with the C corporation is double taxation, where earnings are taxed once when reported by the corporation, and again when dividends are received by its shareholders. This problem is solved by the S corporation, where all items of income, deduction, credit, gain, and loss pass directly through to the entity's shareholders, who then pay all taxes on their own income tax returns. An additional benefit is that the shareholders gain protection from the creditors of the corporation, as would be the case with a C corporation. Further, the 20% business income deduction referred to earlier for sole proprietorships and partnerships is also available to S corporation shareholders through 2025. In this section, we discuss the features, issues, and opportunities associated with S corporations.

Requirements to Form an S Corporation

In order to form an S corporation, an entity must have the following characteristics:

- *Shareholder count*. It can have no more than 100 shareholders. However, it is possible to circumvent this rule by forming a partnership that is controlled by a number of S corporations.

- *Eligible classifications*. Its shareholders must all come from eligible classifications, which are individuals, decedent's estates, and some types of trusts. An S corporation must be dissolved when this is not the case. Here are several additional clarifications of the shareholder concept:
    - *C corporations*. A C corporation cannot be a shareholder in an S corporation, though an S corporation can own all or part of a C corporation.
    - *Estates*. An estate can be useful as a holding entity for S corporation stock until the recipient of the shares can be converted into an acceptable status that will allow the S corporation to continue. For example, a shareholder leaves her estate to a nonresident alien, which is not allowed under S corporation law; the estate holds the shares until they can be sold to a permitted shareholder.
    - *Non-resident aliens*. Nonresident aliens cannot be shareholders, though resident aliens *can* be shareholders. It is also not acceptable for the nonresident alien spouse of a U.S. shareholder to have a current ownership interest in an S corporation.
    - *Partnerships*. A partnership cannot be a shareholder in an S corporation, though an S corporation can be a partner in a partnership.
    - *Trusts*. Only a grantor trust, Section 678 trust, testamentary trust, voting trust, electing small business trust, or qualified subchapter S trust can own shares in an S corporation. A foreign trust, charitable remainder trust, and charitable lead trust *cannot* own shares in an S corporation.

- *Classes of stock*. An S corporation can only have one class of stock, which means that it cannot have preferred stock.

Payroll Tax Reduction

One of the key advantages of an S corporation is being able to avoid some payroll tax on distributions to shareholders. The most common scenario is for a person to be an employee of an S corporation as well as its shareholder. This person wants to maximize her net after-tax income, and so elects to reduce the amount she is being paid as a salary through the S corporation, instead choosing to take the income of the entity as pass-through income that is not subject to any payroll tax. The following example illustrates the concept.

EXAMPLE

Sarah Buckley is the only shareholder of Infinite Solutions, Inc., which is an S corporation. In the current year, Sarah receives a salary from the corporation of $80,000, on which she pays payroll taxes of $6,120 (which is a tax rate of 7.65%). In addition, the corporation pays its share of these taxes, which is another $6,120, for a total of $12,240. If Sarah instead reduces her salary to $60,000 and takes an additional $20,000 as a profit distribution (which still totals her current income of $80,000), then she and the business (combined) will save $3,060 in payroll taxes (calculated as $20,000 × 15.3%). The savings is due to S corporation distributions not being treated as earned income.

Based on this analysis, the most cost-beneficial arrangement would be to take zero compensation from the business and shift all income to the shareholder as a distribution, thereby avoiding all payroll taxes. To avoid this situation, the IRS has mandated that a shareholder who operates a business must take a reasonable salary. In addition, if a family member renders services to an S corporation, reasonable compensation must be provided to that person before the remaining income is allocated to stock held by other family members.

Shareholder Basis

In an S corporation, the stock basis of one's investment starts with the initial cost of the stock purchased. Stock basis is increased by the income received and decreased (but not below zero) by any loss, deductions or distributions received from the corporation.

EXAMPLE

A shareholder invests $100,000 in an S corporation and receives stock in exchange for this investment. After one year, she adds to this her apportionment of the corporation's rental income, interest income, and tax-exempt interest, while deducting the distribution made by the corporation to her. This results in the following calculation of her end-of-period basis:

Beginning of year stock basis	$100,000
Additions:	
Rental income	5,000
Interest income	3,000
Tax-exempt interest	1,000
Reductions:	
Shareholder distribution	-15,000
Stock basis before loss and deductions	94,000
Ordinary income (loss)	-7,000
End of year stock basis	$87,000

Shareholders also get basis in any debt that they personally loan to the S corporation. Any debt loaned from third parties to the corporation does not increase the debt basis of the shareholder.

Shareholders can deduct losses and deductions that exceed their stock basis in the current year against their existing debt basis. This basis is decreased by repayments made by the corporation to the shareholder, and increased by additional loans made to the company by the shareholder.

EXAMPLE

A shareholder loans $30,000 to an S corporation. His debt basis at the beginning of the year is $30,000. During the year, the shareholder deducts $4,000 for S corporation losses that were in excess of the stock basis, and repayments made of debt to the shareholder during the year were $2,000. This results in the following calculation of his end-of-year basis:

Beginning of year debt basis	$30,000
Reductions:	
Principal paid to shareholder	-2,000
Losses in excess of stock basis	-4,000
End of year debt basis	$24,000

Guaranteeing the payment of an S corporation's loan does not increase the basis of a shareholder in any debt, unless the shareholder actually makes a payment to fulfill the terms of the guaranty – at which time it is treated as a loan made directly to the corporation by the shareholder.

Income Distributions

The income of an S corporation is passed through to its shareholders, who then pay taxes on that income on their individual tax returns. The precise tax consequences of a tax distribution will depend on whether the distribution is being made in cash or other property. If appreciated property is distributed to shareholders, then the corporation recognizes a gain and then passes it through to shareholders, who are taxed on the gain.

When an S corporation makes a distribution despite having no reported earnings, the distributions are tax free to the shareholders to the extent of their basis in the S corporation's stock. If the distribution exceeds the amount of their basis, then the excess is accounted for as a capital gain. This gain may be classified as short-term or long-term, depending on how long each shareholder has held the stock. Thus, each shareholder needs to track the amount of basis in all shares held.

Property Distributions

There may be cases in which an S corporation distributes appreciated property to its shareholders. When this distribution is non-liquidating, the distribution is accounted for as though the property had been sold to the shareholders at its fair market value. This gain is then passed through to the shareholders. The shareholders' basis in the property will be at its fair market value.

EXAMPLE

Industrial Landscaping, an S corporation that is 100% owned by Richard Mayhew, distributes to Mayhew the common stock of a publicly-traded company, which it has owned for several years. Industrial's basis in the stock is $42,000, and as of the transfer date, its fair market value was $60,000. Mayhew's basis in the stock will now be $60,000. Also, as the sole shareholder of Industrial, Mr. Mayhew will realize an $18,000 long-term gain.

Sale of S Corporation Stock

When a shareholder of an S corporation sells his or her stock in it, a gain or loss is recognized on the difference between the amount paid to the shareholder for the stock and the person's basis in that stock. Generally, the gain or loss generated from this sale will result in a capital gain or loss.

The selling shareholder's basis is typically adjusted at year-end for the amount of income or loss passed through to the shareholder, as well as the amount of any distributions made by the corporation. This can cause a problem when the business is not sold at year-end, since the shareholder will not know the precise amount of these adjustments until the year-end books have been closed.

Termination of S Corporation Status

An S corporation can lose its status in one of three ways, which are as follows:

- *Passive investment-related termination.* It may generate more than 25% passive income in each of the last three tax years, while also having accumulated earnings and profits at the end of each of those years.
- *Statutory failure.* It may breach one of the statutory requirements for being an S corporation, such as by having more than 100 shareholders, issuing a second class of stock, or taking on a nonresident alien as a shareholder.
- *Voluntary revocation.* Its shareholders may choose to voluntarily revoke its S corporation status. This change takes place when those shareholders holding more than 50% of the outstanding shares consent to the revocation, and a revocation notice is filed with the IRS.

In each of these cases, a revocation of S corporation status (intentional or otherwise) will convert the entity into a C corporation. When an S corporation is terminated, its tax year ends on the same day. This does not mean that the entity closes its books at that point. Instead, it continues recording business transactions, and then allocates income, losses, and so forth between the short year for the S corporation and the following short year for the successor C corporation, based on the number of days in each year.

EXAMPLE

Argot Corporation, an S corporation with a calendar year, terminates its S corporation status as of July 1. Doing so leaves it with an S corporation short year that spans the period January 1 through June 30, while the successor C corporation's short year runs from July 1 to December 31. A perusal of its books reveals that Argot experienced a loss of $80,000 in the first half of the year and a profit of $200,000 in the second half, which was net income of $120,000 for the entire year. Since the results of the corporation are being prorated between the two short years, $60,000 of income will be reported in each short year.

A variation is to conduct the allocation based on normal accounting rules. This approach is only allowed if all shareholders agree to it. Under this approach, the firm reports all items of income, loss, deduction, or credit based on its books and records. This means that the various items to be allocated will be split based on *when* they occurred during the tax year. In the previous example, the use of normal accounting rules would have resulted in a loss of $80,000 being allocated to the S corporation short year, and a gain of $200,000 being allocated to the C corporation short year.

If the shareholders did not intend to terminate the S corporation status of a business, they can still take remediation steps to restore the S corporation status within a reasonable period of time, and then notify the IRS that these steps have been taken. The notification should include an explanation of the event causing the termination, how the event was discovered, when it was discovered, and the steps taken to remediate the situation. Conversely, if the shareholders intended to revoke the S corporation status, then they must wait five years before they can once again elect to convert to that status, or else apply to the IRS for permission to make an earlier election. The IRS is more likely to give permission for an earlier election when the events causing the termination were not within the control of the business or its shareholders.

S Corporation Liquidation

When an S corporation is liquidated, the amounts distributed to its shareholders are treated as full payment in exchange for stock. As part of this transaction, the entity recognizes a gain or loss on property distributions. This gain or loss is calculated as though the corporation had sold its assets to the company's shareholders at fair market value as of the liquidation date. The shareholders' basis in the assets distributed to them as part of the liquidation is their fair market value. In addition, their stock basis will increase or decrease based on the gain or loss recognized when they receive these assets.

EXAMPLE

Sombrero Corporation is a calendar-year S corporation that has been in business for four years. It has one shareholder, Allen Quartermain. Sombrero purchased a ranch for $500,000 immediately upon its incorporation as an investment. Four years later, Sombrero's only asset is the ranch, which now has a fair market value of $900,000 and a cost basis of $500,000. At the end of the current calendar year, Quartermain's basis in his stock is $350,000. Sombrero then liquidates and distributes the ranch to Quartermain, along with the $400,000 gain on the liquidation (calculated as the $900,000 fair market value minus the $500,000 basis), which is a long-term capital gain (given the long holding period). This means that Quartermain's basis has now increased to $750,000 (calculated as the original basis of $350,000 plus the $400,000 gain). When Quartermain receives the ranch on liquidation that has a fair market value of $900,000, he will recognize an additional $150,000 gain (calculated as $900,000 fair market value minus $750,000 of basis). This additional gain is also classified as a long-term capital gain, since he held the stock for more than one year.

If a shareholder of an S corporation does not have sufficient basis to take losses arising from the entity's operations, and the corporation then liquidates, then those unused losses are lost forever as of the liquidation date.

The Annual S Corporation Tax Return

Every S corporation must file the annual Form 1120S information return, which is due by the 15th day of the third month following the close of the entity's tax year. An essential element of this filing is the Schedule K-1, which states each shareholder's portion of the items stated on the Form 1120S. One copy of this schedule must be delivered to each shareholder on or before the filing due date for the return.

The Schedule K-1 is used to pass profits and losses through to the shareholders of an S corporation. When the amount passed through is a loss, the receiving shareholder can use the loss on his or her return only up to the amount of the individual's basis in the stock, and then debt. If the debt basis had already been reduced by prior losses, then it must first be restored before any adjustments are made to the shareholder's basis in the stock.

EXAMPLE

Ellen Driskell is a 30% shareholder in Smithy Ironworks, which is an S corporation. Ms. Driskell's basis in her stock is $28,000. Also, she issues a loan to the company in which her basis is $75,000. In the current year, her share of the corporation's pass-through loss is $35,000. She can deduct the entire $35,000 amount, which will reduce her stock basis to zero and her loan basis to $68,000.

In the following year, the firm passes through $10,000 of profits to her. This increases her debt basis back to $75,000, while also increasing her stock basis by $3,000.

Advantages and Disadvantages

The advantages of an S corporation are:

- *Asset contributions*. Under certain conditions, a taxpayer can contribute assets to an S corporation, tax free.
- *Create capital gains with borrowed funds*. A business may want to create capital gains in order to offset capital losses that would otherwise have to be carried forward. One way to do so uses the unique structure of an S corporation, where *any* distribution in excess of a shareholder's basis will generate capital gains. This can be done by having the S corporation borrow money (probably secured by company assets) and then distribute the borrowed funds to the shareholder. As long as this distribution exceeds the shareholder's basis, it is considered a capital gain, and so can be used to offset the shareholder's capital loss.
- *Distribute appreciated property*. A distribution of appreciated property by an S corporation to its shareholders generates a gain in the amount of the difference between the corporation's basis in the asset and its fair market value. This gain increases the basis of the shareholders' stock in the corporation.
- *Distributions are free of payroll taxes*. Any distributions made from an S corporation to shareholders are not subject to payroll taxes. This means that social security, unemployment, and Medicare taxes are not paid on these distributions.
- *Double taxation circumvention*. The earnings of an S corporation are only taxed once, at the level of its shareholders. This is significantly better than for a C corporation, where the corporation is taxed and then again when any distributions to shareholders are taxed.
- *Immediate loss deductions*. It is especially useful to employ an S corporation for a startup business, since the usual startup losses can be deducted, though it is capped at the amount of the shareholder's basis in the corporation's stock and the amount of any loans to it. Any losses in excess of the shareholder's basis can be rolled forward to a later period, when the shareholder's basis may have increased.
- *No accumulated earnings tax*. An S corporation is not subject to the accumulated earnings tax, which applies to a C corporation if it accumulates an excessive amount of earnings without paying some portion of it to shareholders.
- *Passive loss offsets*. If a shareholder does not actively participate in managing the business, any income passed through from it is characterized as passive, and so can be used to offset passive losses.
- *Shareholder protection*. As is the case with any corporation, an S corporation shields its shareholders from the debts of the corporation.
- *Single taxation level on sale of business*. When an S corporation is sold, the shareholders will pay tax on the distribution. This is better than for a C corporation, where tax is paid by the corporation and again by the shareholders when the proceeds are forwarded to them.

For these reasons, an S corporation might be especially useful when the firm is likely to incur large losses and credits, since they can be passed through to and more profitably used by shareholders. It can also be useful when a business does not need to accumulate much capital, as is frequently the case with a services-based or Internet business that needs little working capital or fixed assets; this is because distributions will likely need to be made to the shareholders, so that they can pay for their respective shares of the corporation's taxes. In addition, the S corporation structure is useful when the business may generate liabilities from which its shareholders want to be shielded.

The disadvantages of an S corporation are:

- *Fiscal year*. An S corporation has to report on a calendar-year basis, unless it can establish a business purpose for reporting on some other basis. The firm must pay the IRS a deposit when it uses any other date range as its fiscal year (which is still limited to a year-end of September 30, October 31, or November 30). This deposit is intended to approximate the amount of tax that would be paid if the corporation changed to a calendar year; thus, the payments offset the income tax deferral provided by the fiscal year.
- *Method of accounting*. An S corporation cannot adopt a method of accounting that differs from the method previously used when it was a C corporation, unless it first gains the assent of the IRS.
- *Minimal cash retention*. It is difficult for an S corporation to build up cash reserves, since its shareholders need distributions in order to pay taxes on the income that has been passed through to them.
- *Net operating loss carryforwards*. It is not allowable to carry forward net operating losses (NOLs) from a C corporation to an S corporation, which can be a significant concern when an NOL is quite large.
- *Passive investment income*. When a C corporation converts to an S corporation, it may fail the test if it had gross receipts of more than 25% from passive investment income in each of the past three years. The C corporation can eliminate this problem by declaring a dividend prior to the S corporation election that flushes out this income.
- *Record keeping*. The S corporation accountant must maintain records for the basis in its shareholders' stock, which is needed to determine the taxability of distributions.
- *Taxable built-in gains*. A tax is imposed if an S corporation sells or distributes to its shareholders any assets that appreciated in value before the firm converted to an S corporation. The tax applies to any asset sales or distributions that arose during the five years prior to the date of the conversion to an S corporation.
- *Tax-free fringe benefits*. Some tax-free fringe benefits (such as accident and health insurance premiums) are not available to the shareholders in an S corporation that hold more than a 2% interest in the business. When an S

corporation pays for these benefits, they are treated as wages, which means that payroll taxes will be applied to them.

- *Unplanned termination.* A dissident shareholder can trigger the termination of the entity's S status by transferring shares to an entity that is not allowed to be a shareholder, such as a nonresident alien.

EXAMPLE

Bunyan Corporation is initially organized as a C corporation. During its first three years in business, it accumulated a net operating loss of $180,000. Its owners then elect to switch it to an S corporation. Bunyan cannot use the NOL for as long as the entity remains an S corporation. During its time as an S corporation, each year counts toward the 20-year limitation on how long the NOL can be used. If the firm does not terminate its S corporation status before the 20 years are up, then it can never use the NOL.

The preceding issues will generally not prevent shareholders from converting to an S corporation, but they should be aware of these issues in advance and plan for them accordingly, in order to mitigate their effects.

Business Type Comparison

The following two exhibits present a comparison of the organizational structures that we have just discussed, focusing on such matters as the number of allowed owners, the income tax brackets used, and whether multiple classes of stock are allowed. The high degree of variability among these choices allows one to select a structure that most closely aligns with the needs of a business. For example:

- *Small family-owned business.* Might opt for an S corporation, due to the limited number of shareholders allowed and the protection from liability.
- *Professional service provider.* Might choose a personal service corporation in order to pay lower taxes, shelter under its liability protection, and benefit from the tax deductibility of fringe benefit expenditures.
- *Rapidly growing business.* Might opt for a C corporation in order to raise money by selling shares to many shareholders.
- *Real estate investment.* Might opt to raise capital to construct a building with a limited partnership arrangement, since it protects the limited partners from creditors to some degree.

Comparison of Organizational Structures: S Corp., C Corp., and Partnership

Issue	S Corporation	C Corporation	General Partnership
Number of owners	Limited to 100 shareholders	Unlimited number of shareholders	Unlimited number of partners
Types of shareholders	Some restrictions on the types of shareholders	No restriction on the types of shareholders	No restriction on the types of partners
Income tax brackets	The brackets of the shareholders are used	A 21% income tax is imposed on the corporation	The brackets of the partners are used
Ease of formation	Subject to IRS approval	Easy	Easy, but should write a partnership agreement
Protection from creditors	Yes	Yes	No protection from creditors for the partners
Classes of stock allowed	One	Multiple	Based on percentage of ownership
Double taxation	No – income and losses pass through to shareholders	Yes – applies to any dividends paid to shareholders	No – income and losses pass through to partners
Self-employment taxes applied to owners	Only on compensation paid for services rendered; the remainder is a distribution that is free of payroll taxes	Only on compensation paid for services rendered	All distributions are subject to self-employment tax
Owners can participate in management	Yes	Yes	Yes

Comparison of Organizational Structures: Limited Partnership and Limited Liability Company

Issue	Sole Proprietorship	Limited Partnership	Limited Liability Company
Number of owners	One	Must have at least one general partner and one limited partner	Unlimited number of members
Types of shareholders	Individual	No limitation on the types of partners	No restriction on the types of members
Income tax brackets	The brackets of the owner are used	The brackets of the partners are used	The brackets of the members are used
Ease of formation	Very easy, since is not a separate entity	Some difficulty, depending on the rules of the applicable state government	Relatively easy, but should write an LLC agreement
Protection from creditors	Not at all; the owner is liable for the obligations of the business	Only for the limited partners, who are at risk for the amount of their investments in the entity	Yes, except for cases where professional malpractice applies
Classes of stock allowed	Not applicable, since there are no shares	Not applicable, since limited partners have no voting rights	An LLC is structured so that the owners each have a membership interest in the company, not stock
Double taxation	No	No	No
Self-employment taxes applied to owners	The entity is not separable from the owner, so in effect the owner pays self-employment taxes	Only applies to the general partner	Yes, if it is a service partnership where the members cannot be classified as limited partners
Owners can participate in management	The owner is the manager	Only those classified as general partners	Yes

Summary

The diversity of available entity types presents the business owner with a broad array of options. When selecting which one to use, it can be helpful to also plan for the future, when the organization may need to be configured somewhat differently. For example, does a small business start off as an S corporation and then switch to a C corporation in order to raise more money and/or go public? Or perhaps a firm begins as a sole proprietorship and then needs to add owners, possibly resulting in a general or limited partnership. In short, select an entity type that not only fits your current needs, but which will also be able to transition into whatever is needed to meet the organization's needs in later years.

Glossary

A

Accrual basis of accounting. When accounting transactions for revenue are recorded when earned and expenses when they are incurred.

Active trade. When a business has begun the conduct of operations for which it was organized.

D

Double taxation. When the earnings of a corporation are taxed, and the dividends it distributes to shareholders are also taxed at the shareholder level.

F

First-in, first out method. The tracking of inventory based on the concept that the first items to enter inventory are the first ones to be used.

H

Hobby activity. An activity performed for recreation or pleasure, not with the intent to earn a consistent profit.

Hot assets. Accounts receivable not already recognized as income, LIFO reserves, appreciated inventory, and depreciation recapture.

I

Inside basis. A partnership's tax basis on individual assets.

Investigatory expenses. Expenses related to investigating the creation or acquisition of a trade or business.

L

Last-in, first-out method. The tracking of inventory based on the concept that the last items to enter inventory are the first ones to be used.

O

Original basis. The amount of money contributed by a partner to a partnership.

Outside basis. The tax basis of each individual partner's interest in a partnership.

S

Start-up costs. Those costs paid or incurred in connection with investigating the creation or acquisition of an active trade or business, or creating an active trade or business.

Index